Natural Disasters

Terrifying Tornadoes

Julie Richards

Chelsea House Publishers
1974 Sproul Road, Suite 400
Broomall, PA 19008-0914

The Chelsea House world wide web address is www.chelseahouse.com

Library of Congress Cataloging-in-Publication Data Applied for.

ISBN 0-7910-6579-0

First published in 2001 by
Macmillan Education Australia Pty Ltd
627 Chapel Street, South Yarra, Australia 3141

Copyright © Julie Richards 2001

Edited by Sally Woollett
Text design by Polar Design Pty Ltd
Cover design by Polar Design Pty Ltd
Illustrations and maps by Pat Kermode, Purple Rabbit Productions
Printed in Hong Kong

Acknowledgements
The author and the publisher are grateful to the following for permission to reproduce copyright material:

Cover photograph: Tornado funnel, courtesy of Australian Picture Library/Sharpshooters.

AP/AAP, p. 29 (bottom); Australian Picture Library/CORBIS, pp. 11, 22 (top), 23 (top), 28; Australian Picture Library/Premium Stock Photography GMB, p. 26; Australian Picture Library/Sharpshooters, p. 4; Bureau of Meteorology, pp. 5 (bottom), 20 (top), 21 (bottom), 22 (bottom), 23 (bottom), 27 (top); Bureau of Meteorology/Imagery from the Japan Meteorological Agency Geostationary Satellite, p. 21 (top); Bureau of Meteorology/Peter Mudra, p. 14; Corbis Digital Stock, p. 9; CP/AP/AAP, p. 29 (top); National Oceanic and Atmospheric Administration/Department of Commerce/Mr. Paul Huffman, p. 5 (top); NOAA Photo Library, NOAA Central Library, pp. 10 (bottom), 17 (top), 18, 20 (bottom), 24, 25; PhotoDisc, pp. 2, 3, 10 (top), 15, 31, 32; Photolibrary.com, pp. 7, 16–17.

While every care has been taken to trace and acknowledge copyright the publishers tender their apologies for any accidental infringement where copyright has proved untraceable. Where the attempt has been unsuccessful, the publisher welcomes information that would redress the situation.

Contents

The fastest wind
on Earth

Can you imagine a **wind spinning** at more than
400 kilometers (250 miles) an hour?

A **wind so powerful** that it can **lift** and **throw** something
as heavy as a train, carry houses away,
and even **tear** the bark from trees?

If you have ever been in the path of a tornado,
you might have seen this happen.

TORNADOES are the
most violent windstorms known
to happen on Earth.

You might have read about
these things in a newspaper.
Or perhaps you have watched
a television news report or
documentary program, where
people talked about what
happened when a tornado hit
the area in which they live.

Every year, tornadoes cause
incredible damage to homes
and people's belongings. They
destroy crops and kill or injure
many people. This is why a
tornado is often called a natural
disaster.

What is a tornado?

A tornado is a fiercely spinning tube of air that hangs from the bottom of a thunderstorm **cloud**. When it touches the ground, it acts like a giant vacuum cleaner, sucking up everything in its path. Tornadoes are very dangerous and you should never get close to one.

Some thunderstorms can produce more than one tornado at the same time. In the town of Wichita Falls in the United States of America (USA), three tornadoes joined together to form one giant tornado. Twenty thousand people lost their homes. Surprisingly, only 44 people were killed. As many as six separate tornadoes have been seen to drop from a single thunderstorm!

These twin tornadoes tore through Elkhart, Indiana, USA on Palm Sunday in 1965.

A tornado was probably responsible for tearing a path through this forest in Tasmania, Australia.

Disaster Detective

Tornadoes are also called twisters.
Can you find out why?

An unseen tornado

Sometimes a big tornado will not be seen by anyone. In Australia, nobody saw the tornado that swept through northern New South Wales in January, 1970. However, it was not too difficult to see where it had been. The tornado had travelled through a forest and knocked down nearly one million trees!

Where do tornadoes happen?

Tornadoes have been reported in most parts of the world. You may already know about an area in the USA known as Tornado Alley. This is where most of the world's tornadoes happen.

Lots of warm, moist air flows up from the Gulf of Mexico. At the same time, lots of cold, dry air moves down from Canada. Both lots of air **collide** above Tornado Alley. With no mountain ranges in between to slow them down, they mix together very quickly and violently to form huge, whirling thunderstorms.

Australia has plenty of wide, open spaces too, but not many people live in these parts. This means that tornadoes can happen without anyone knowing about them. It also means there is less danger. However, more people live in Tornado Alley. Sometimes a tornado will destroy nearly a whole town, killing and injuring many people.

cool dry air

warm moist air

SOUTH DAKOTA
NEBRASKA
IOWA
ILLINOIS
INDIANA
KANSAS
MISSOURI
OKLAHOMA
ARKANSAS
MISSISSIPPI
GEORGIA
ALABAMA
TEXAS
LOUISIANA
FLORIDA

Most of the world's tornadoes happen in Tornado Alley, USA.

Disaster Detective

Find out if there are other parts of the world that are flat and open like Tornado Alley or Australia. You might like to find out if they have tornadoes, too.

Tornado tricks

Tornadoes have been seen to do some amazing things. Once a tornado gets going, even something as big as a mountain cannot always stop it. Of course, a tornado cannot blow a mountain away, but some have been seen to climb up and down mountains. Other tornadoes have travelled into deep canyons. One even dropped over a cliff onto the town below.

When do tornadoes happen?

Although tornadoes can happen just about anywhere at any time, they are more frequent at certain times of the year.

Tornadoes usually occur during late spring or early summer. Most will happen between noon and midnight, after the temperature has reached its maximum for the day. To understand why this is important, we need to look at our **atmosphere** more closely.

Tornadoes and whirlwinds such as these happen in the spring in Kansas, USA.

How do tornadoes form?

The atmosphere

The atmosphere is a blanket of air surrounding the Earth. It is where all of the world's weather happens. Shining through the atmosphere, the Sun's energy drives air and water around our entire planet by creating wind and clouds.

Each day the ground soaks up warmth from the sunshine. When this happens, the air just above the ground is warmed. Some parts will be warmed more quickly than others will. For example, a shady forest will take much longer to heat up than a place that has no shade. Air that is warmed quickly becomes lighter and begins to rise. Cooler, heavier air rushes in to fill the space it leaves behind. When cool air and warm air move like this we call it wind.

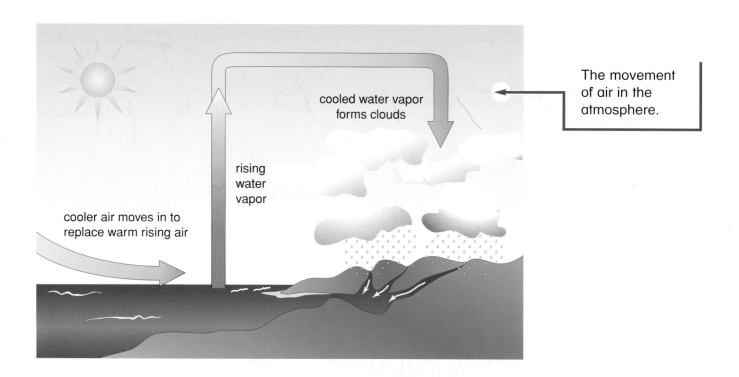

cooled water vapor forms clouds

rising water vapor

cooler air moves in to replace warm rising air

The movement of air in the atmosphere.

Clouds

Clouds are made up of millions of tiny droplets of water floating through the air. When the sun warms the ground it also warms the oceans, lakes and rivers. Some of the water changes into an invisible gas called water vapor. Rising warm air carries the water vapor high up into the colder air above. The air and the water vapor soon begin to cool. As it cools, the water vapor changes back into tiny droplets. This is called **condensation**. The groups of water droplets that can be seen in the sky when this happens are called clouds.

Cumulus clouds are light and puffy.

Thunderclouds

Thunderstorms can grow from those big, puffy white cumulus clouds that you often see on a summer afternoon. Clouds appear to be white because the water droplets they are made of reflect sunlight. As a cumulus cloud becomes thicker and heavier with droplets, it darkens because sunlight cannot pass through it. It then becomes a cumulonimbus or thundercloud.

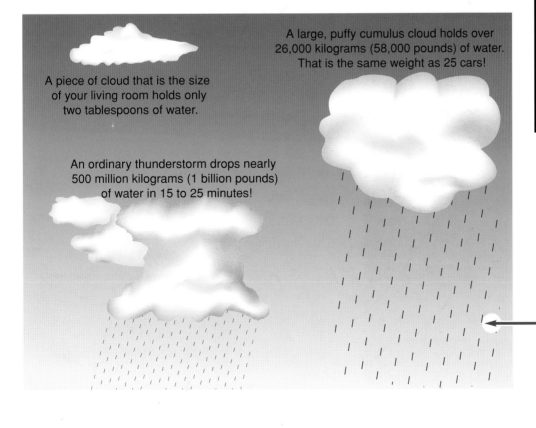

A large, puffy cumulus cloud holds over 26,000 kilograms (58,000 pounds) of water. That is the same weight as 25 cars!

A piece of cloud that is the size of your living room holds only two tablespoons of water.

An ordinary thunderstorm drops nearly 500 million kilograms (1 billion pounds) of water in 15 to 25 minutes!

Different sized clouds hold different amounts of water.

Which thunderclouds produce tornadoes?

Right now, there are nearly 2,000 thunderstorms happening in different parts of the world. Within these thunderclouds, warm air and water vapor are rushing up to the cooler top part of the cloud and changing back into water droplets. Sometimes some of the air and water vapor goes so high that it gets cold enough to turn into ice crystals. There is so much air rushing around inside the cloud that ice crystals and water droplets keep crashing into one another. Each time they collide they join together. Eventually, they become too heavy to stay inside the cloud and fall back to the ground as **hailstones** and raindrops.

Special thunderstorms called supercells are able to make tornadoes.

Can you see the rain falling from this thundercloud?

Soon, the heavier cooler air smothers the rising warm air in much the same way that a fire hose drowns the flames of a fire. Without rising warm air to feed it, the thunderstorm dies.

Most thunderstorms are small and weak and not capable of producing tornadoes. It takes a very special type of thunderstorm called a **supercell** to make a tornado.

> ### GUESS WHAT?
> Only about one thunderstorm in 1,000 produces a tornado.

How a tornado grows inside a supercell thunderstorm

Supercell thunderstorms have one thing that ordinary thunderstorms do not—something called **wind shear**.

Wind shear

Have you ever noticed that sometimes a gentle breeze is blowing just enough to rustle the leaves of nearby trees, yet the clouds are racing across the sky in a different direction? This is because the clouds are being moved about by a higher, faster wind than the trees on the ground. This is wind shear.

Wind socks show us how fast the wind above is blowing.

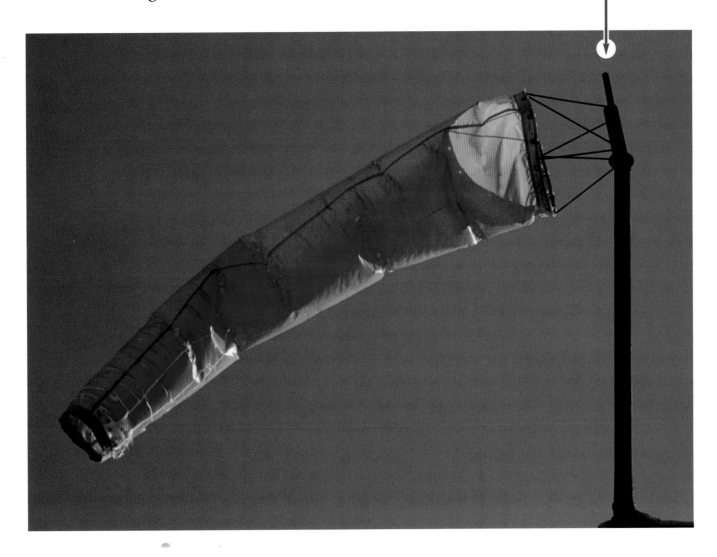

How wind shear helps a tornado to grow

In a smaller space like a thundercloud these different types of winds are much closer together. As they pass each other in different directions the air caught in between them starts to spin.

The **vortex** inside the thunderstorm stretches into a tube until it hangs below the thundercloud. When this happens it is called a **funnel cloud**. A funnel cloud is not a tornado until it touches the ground below.

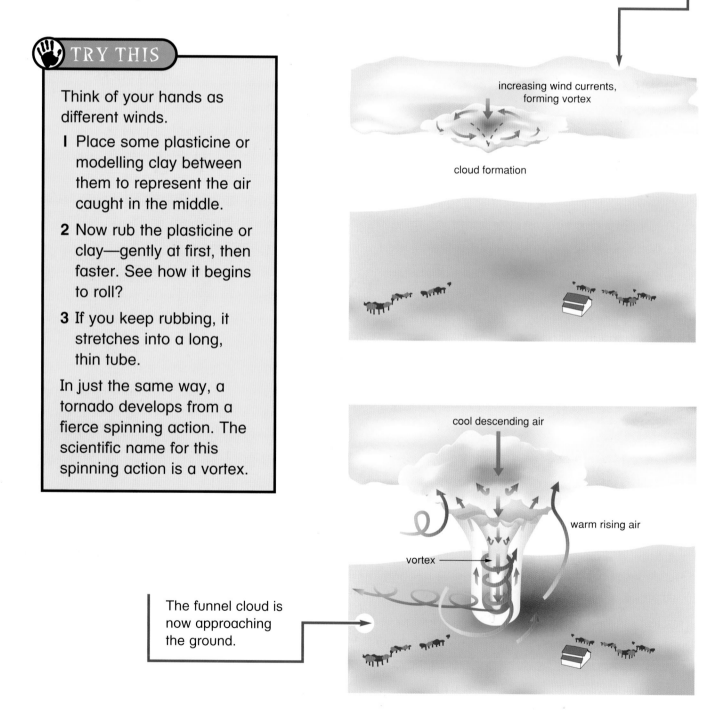

How a vortex forms inside a thundercloud.

increasing wind currents, forming vortex

cloud formation

cool descending air

warm rising air

vortex

The funnel cloud is now approaching the ground.

🖐 TRY THIS

Think of your hands as different winds.

1 Place some plasticine or modelling clay between them to represent the air caught in the middle.

2 Now rub the plasticine or clay—gently at first, then faster. See how it begins to roll?

3 If you keep rubbing, it stretches into a long, thin tube.

In just the same way, a tornado develops from a fierce spinning action. The scientific name for this spinning action is a vortex.

Tornado touchdown!

Before touchdown

Thunderstorms that produce tornadoes also make a lot of lightning, thunder, rain and large hailstones.

Once this noisy first part of the thunderstorm passes, it can become so quiet that you may think the storm has finished. It is during this time that the tornado will be growing inside the back part of the thundercloud. If the cloud above you begins to dip and swirl it means that the vortex is stretching downwards inside the storm. Soon the funnel cloud will appear.

Can you see the funnel cloud in this thundercloud?

Touchdown!

FUNNEL FACTS

- ☑ Most funnels are between 10 meters and 400 meters wide. The tornado that ripped through that northern New South Wales forest had a funnel 1.6 kilometers (one mile) wide!

- ☑ Wide funnels are usually cone shaped.

- ☑ Narrow funnels look like elephant trunks.

- ☑ A narrow funnel can be just as deadly as a wide one.

- ☑ Most funnels get their color from the dirt they suck up.

Touching down

When a funnel cloud reaches the ground it is known as **touchdown**. People who have watched a tornado touch down often remember hearing a loud, roaring noise like a passing train or a jumbo jet. The closer to the ground the funnel cloud gets, the louder the roar. This is not surprising because lots of dirt, rocks and other things are being sucked up and tossed around inside the whirling funnel.

On the ground

Once on the ground, the tornado stays attached to the thundercloud above. It is very difficult to know which way tornadoes will move. Sometimes they can change direction suddenly.

Tornadoes do not travel very fast—up to 100 kilometers (70 miles) per hour. It is the twisting winds of the tornado's funnel that cause the terrible damage. These winds can blow at up to speeds of 500 kilometers (312 miles) per hour!

In the **Southern Hemisphere**, where Australia is, most tornadoes spin **clockwise**. In the USA, and other countries in the **Northern Hemisphere**, tornadoes usually spin **counterclockwise**.

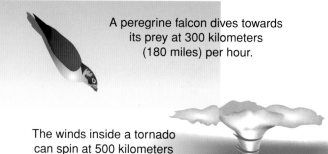

A peregrine falcon dives towards its prey at 300 kilometers (180 miles) per hour.

The winds inside a tornado can spin at 500 kilometers (312 miles) per hour.

A jumbo jet flies at 920 kilometers (580 miles) per hour.

Disaster Detective

The longest track left by a tornado was measured at 471 kilometers (292 miles). Perhaps you can find some other record-breaking tornado measurements.

The winds inside a tornado spin very fast.

Funnel clouds are usually a blue-grey color. Once they touch the ground and begin sucking up dirt and rocks, their color changes to brown or black.

What kinds of damage can a tornado do?

When a tornado moves over an object such as a house, the racing, twisting winds of the funnel smash into it from all sides at once. No wonder the house seems to explode into a million pieces in just seconds! These pieces or fragments are called **debris**.

The winds of a tornado do a lot of damage.

GUESS WHAT?

The whirling of a tornado's funnel produces enough electricity to power a medium-sized city. The thunderstorm above the tornado is 40,000 times more powerful. One flash of lightning could keep a light bulb burning for 3 months.

Inside the funnel

The air in the funnel is constantly spinning upwards. As it does so, it sucks up the debris. The faster the air spins, the more sucking power the tornado has. Now you can see why some tornadoes can lift large animals, cars and even houses.

Read All About It!

Kansas farmer sees inside a tornado and lives!

Will Keller is the only person to have seen inside a tornado. As the funnel lifted from the ground, the lightning allowed Will to see the clouds spinning around its center. He said that the air was very still inside, that the end of the funnel made a loud hissing noise and there was a burning, gassy smell that made it difficult for him to breathe.

Dangerous flying objects

Everything the funnel sucks up will later be thrown out again. The tornado collects debris from the ground and sprays it in all directions, just like a machine-gun.

Not all of these pieces or fragments will be the same size. The debris could be rocks, parts of buildings or cars, plants or trees, or just the dirt on the ground. Tornadoes have even peeled the asphalt from roads.

All of these fragments are sucked into the funnel and whirled around with the wind. As long as the rising air is strong enough to hold the fragments up, the tornado can carry them long distances before spitting them out.

Debris picked up by this tornado was found up to 96 kilometers (60 miles) from the town.

Strange flying objects

- A sleeping baby was lifted from its cradle, carried through the air and placed safely on the ground hundreds of meters away, still fast asleep!

- A cupboard containing glasses and china plates was sucked into a funnel and then set down on the ground again. Nothing inside the cupboard was broken.

- A herd of very confused horses was left sitting on top of a barn roof.

You might think that large fragments are more dangerous than small ones. However, it is usually small things travelling extremely fast that are most dangerous. A piece of straw might seem small and weak. That same piece of straw can easily kill a person or an animal if it is travelling at a speed of 300 kilometers (187 miles) per hour or more. Pieces of straw have been found stuck fast in tree trunks. Even sand and gravel can have the same power as bullets when blown about at high speed.

A tornado caused this plastic record to slice into a telephone pole.

Disaster Detective

There are lots of strange stories about tornadoes. Can fish fall from the sky?

In 1994, it suddenly began raining fish in the Northern Territory, Australia. It is possible that the fish were sucked up by a tornado then dropped when it rained. Even frogs frozen inside hail have come bouncing down. When the hail melted, the frogs hopped away! You might like to collect some stories for yourself.

How long does a tornado last?

Once a tornado has touched down there is nothing anyone can do to stop it. Given the power and speed of tornadoes, what makes them just disappear?

Most tornadoes only last a few minutes. However, even a tornado lasting only a minute can do a lot of damage if it touches down near a town.

Many tornadoes begin to weaken when they cross uneven ground or when a very large obstacle such as a town blocks their path. As a tornado weakens, the funnel becomes thin and straggly and looks like a rippling rope. This is called the decaying or rope stage. Shortly after this, the funnel disappears. Weather scientists call this **dissipation**. Nobody really understands why a tornado disappears when it does.

These pictures show a tornado forming, touching down and then decaying.

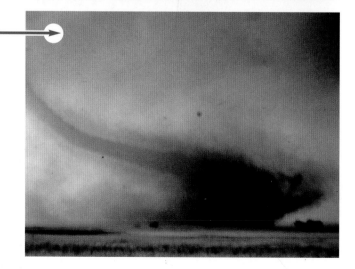

GUESS WHAT?

One tornado that touched down in the Midwest of the USA in 1977 lasted more than seven hours and travelled over 600 kilometers (375 miles).

Forecasting and measuring tornadoes

Scientists who study the weather are called **meteorologists**. Meteorologists use computers, special maps and equipment to try and tell us what sort of weather is coming our way. This is called a prediction or forecast. They want to find a better way of warning people that a tornado might be growing inside a nearby thunderstorm. It might not prevent the damage a tornado causes, but it will help to save lives.

The F Scale

Tornadoes are measured on a scale called the Fujita Pearson Tornado Intensity Scale or **F Scale**. The F Scale is named after the two meteorologists who invented it, Professor T. Theodore Fujita and Allen Pearson. After meteorologists check the damage the tornado has done, they give the tornado a rating from F-0 (weakest) to F-5 (strongest). A tornado stronger than F-5 has not happened yet!

The F Scale

Number	Intensity	Wind speed	Damage
F-0	Gale	65–116 kilometers per hour (40–72 miles per hour)	Breaks tree branches, damages road signs
F-1	Moderate	117–180 kilometers per hour (73–112 miles per hour)	Lifts off roof tiles, pushes cars off the road
F-2	Significant	181–253 kilometers per hour (113–157 miles per hour)	Large trees uprooted, mobile homes destroyed
F-3	Severe	254–332 kilometers per hour (158–206 miles per hour)	Roofs and some walls torn from houses
F-4	Devastating	333–419 kilometers per hour (207–260 miles per hour)	Houses completely destroyed, large missiles such as cars are thrown
F-5	Incredible	418–509 kilometers per hour (261–318 miles per hour)	Strong buildings thrown, into air and destroyed, bark torn from trees

Anemometers

Meteorologists use an instrument called an **anemometer** to measure wind speed. However, the swirling winds of a tornado are so violent that the anemometers used to measure normal wind speed would be torn to pieces.

TOTO

TOTO stands for **TO**table **T**ornado **O**bservatory. TOTO was a very heavy weather station that meteorologists would place in the path of a tornado. Not knowing the direction a tornado would take made it too difficult to get TOTO into the right position. Although some tornadoes came close, none ever passed right over it.

This vane anemometer is designed to measure normal wind speeds.

Turtles

Some meteorologists tried smaller, flatter weather instruments called **turtles**. A number of turtles would be spread over the ground where a tornado might be expected to touch down. Turtles were strong and they also covered more ground than TOTO could. However, knowing where to place the turtles was still a problem.

Measuring tornadoes will always be difficult because meteorologists can never be sure when and where a tornado will touch down.

TOTO was never able to be placed directly in the path of a tornado.

Why are tornadoes so difficult to forecast?

Tornadoes are very different from other winds. Big winds such as hurricanes and cyclones form over the sea. A hurricane or cyclone can take several days to become a very powerful storm, so meteorologists can predict that one is on the way before it reaches land. This means that meteorologists can track the storm and warn anyone who may be in danger.

Tornadoes can grow inside thunderstorms and touch down in as little as five to ten minutes. There is usually little time to warn people of the danger once a tornado is on the ground.

Meteorologists can find out if a hurricane is forming.

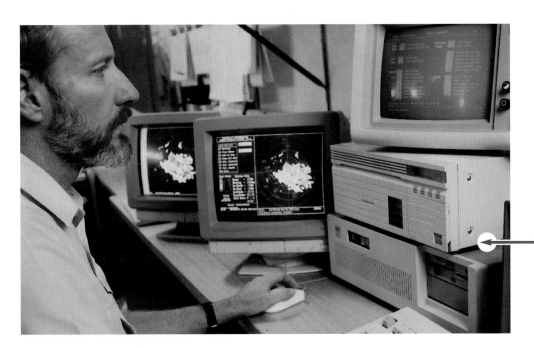

Meteorologists gather information about tornadoes so they can try to predict them.

When severe thunderstorms are expected, a tornado watch will be issued so that everyone is aware that tornadoes are possible. A tornado alert is broadcast on radio and television if one is spotted on the ground.

Big thunderstorms are not the only cause of tornadoes. Sometimes, it is the smaller thunderstorms that cause them. Meteorologists are always searching for more reliable ways of forecasting and measuring tornadoes.

Tornado tracking equipment

Meteorologists work in weather stations. These weather stations form a network around the world, helping meteorologists to swap important information about the weather. All meteorologists are trained to use special equipment to help them track the supercell thunderstorms that might trigger tornadoes.

Satellites

High above the Earth, **satellites** collect information about the world's weather. Satellites have instruments that can measure the air temperature in different parts of the world. They can also see where clouds are forming. The information collected is then sent back to Earth. Computers can change this information into pictures and maps for meteorologists to use when making forecasts.

Radar

Radar sends out a signal that bounces off the hailstones and raindrops inside clouds. This enables meteorologists to track some of the smaller thunderstorms that might be missed by weather stations on the ground.

This is one of a network of weather stations in the United Kingdom.

Information about the weather is gathered using this radar dome.

Radiosondes

A package of weather instruments attached to a weather balloon is called a **radiosonde**. At weather stations all over the world meteorologists release radiosondes each day. Radiosondes check the weather conditions high up in the atmosphere and send back the information. They help meteorologists to learn whether or not conditions are right for supercell thunderstorms to develop.

Doppler radar

Doppler radar is even better than ordinary radar. It can be used to find the spinning air of a tornado while it is still inside the thundercloud. This can give meteorologists more time to warn people that a tornado is on the way.

Releasing a radiosonde.

Storm chasers and storm spotters

Storm chasers

Meteorologists realized a long time ago that if they were to learn more about tornadoes then they would have to get as close as possible to study them. However, meteorologists are not the only people who chase tornadoes. People fascinated by storms and big winds may chase tornadoes as a hobby. These people are called storm chasers. Serious storm chasers write reports describing the tornado and share them with the meteorologists working in special storm laboratories.

Storm spotters

Storm spotters do not actively chase tornadoes. They have the important job of watching out for severe thunderstorms and tornadoes in the area in which they live. When a storm or tornado is sighted, storm spotters contact their nearest weather station or severe storms laboratory. They give important information such as the direction the tornado or storm is travelling in. Meteorologists can use this information to send out a tornado alert or a tornado watch to nearby towns and farms.

Storm chasers often take many photographs of approaching tornadoes.

Skills and equipment

Chasers and spotters have to be able to recognize different types of clouds. Chasers have to be able to make their own weather forecasts as well. Storm chasing can be a very dangerous activity. Chasers need to be aware of certain hazards such as lightning, **flash floods,** flying debris and large hailstones.

The National Severe Storm Laboratory in the USA has mobile laboratories set up for professional storm chasing.

Storm chasers use four-wheel drive vehicles in case they have to escape a tornado or a flood on the main roads. Electricity and mobile phone towers are usually the first things to be damaged during severe thunderstorms, so chasers use radios to communicate. They also have laptop computers, cameras and video equipment to help them record what they see. Many of the spectacular photographs that you have seen in this book were taken with special lenses that make the tornadoes appear closer then they really are. Serious storm chasers always take care and never place themselves or others in danger.

When is a tornado not a tornado?

When it is a …

Gustnado

A **gustnado** is a smaller, weaker spinning tube of air. Gustnadoes can be felt as bursts of whirling wind when a thunderstorm is very close, but they are not connected to the thundercloud itself. Because gustnadoes can pick up dust and small debris and twirl them around, they are often mistaken for tornadoes.

Waterspout

When a tornado crosses water it can become a **waterspout**. A real waterspout is different from a tornado in a number of ways.

➤ It forms over shallow water.

➤ It comes from a different type of cloud.

➤ It is not started by a thunderstorm.

➤ It is usually smaller.

➤ It travels more slowly.

➤ It spins more gently.

The water in a true waterspout actually comes from the moist, spinning air around it, not the sea. It only looks as if the sea is being sucked into the funnel.

GUESS WHAT?

In the past, waterspouts were sometimes mistaken for long-necked sea monsters. Some people still believe that a waterspout lies behind the legend of Scotland's Loch Ness monster.

Landspout

A **landspout** comes from the same type of cloud as a waterspout. However, as its name suggests, a landspout will only happen over dry land. They are mostly smaller and weaker than tornadoes.

Dust devil

A **dust devil** is very different from a tornado because it is never attached to a cloud. Dust devils always begin on the ground. When very hot air rises off a baking surface such as asphalt in a school yard, it mixes with cooler breezes around it. This makes the air swirl upwards, carrying dust and sand with it.

Dust devils often happen on hot days.

Fire devil

A large fire can create its own weather. The intense heat of the flames can pull in very strong gusts of wind, pushing the flames even higher. As the hot air spirals upwards, it causes the flames to twist and spin too, turning it into a fiery whirlwind or **fire devil**.

A large fire devil can be just as powerful as a tornado. It can travel very fast, snapping off tree trunks and picking up burning logs. Smaller burning objects can be carried high into the atmosphere on these strong winds. Fresh fires can be started wherever they finally fall.

> **GUESS WHAT?**
>
> Dust devils are also known as willy-willies or cockeye bobs.

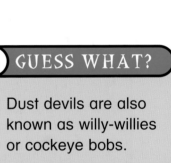

Fire devils can carry a wildfire to other parts of a forest.

Protection from tornadoes

Building tornado-proof houses is too expensive, so the safest place to be when a tornado strikes is underground. Houses, schools and hospitals in tornado areas usually have underground rooms called shelters. Families, workers and students all practice getting into these shelters as quickly and as calmly as possible. This is called a tornado drill.

If there is no underground shelter available, you should go to the smallest room in the house. Always stay low and keep away from any windows or glass doors. Cover yourself with a cushion or mattress to protect your head. If a tornado alert has been given, do not go outside until you know that the danger has passed.

TORNADO FACTS

Tornado shelter checklist

☑ canned food

☑ blankets

☑ bottled water

☑ flashlights

Many homes and public buildings in tornado areas have basements that can be used as shelters.

Disaster Detective

What other useful things could be added to the tornado checklist? Why?

After a tornado

People who help

Doctors, nurses and ambulance officers are just a few of the many people needed to help after a tornado has struck. Some helpers will be volunteers from organizations that train people to do first aid and carry out rescues.

Everybody helps in their own special way. People who live too far away to come and help will often donate money to buy medicine, blankets, food and clothes. Some people even make special teddy bears to give to the children who have been frightened by the tornado.

These rescue workers are searching for survivors of a tornado that touched down near Calgary, Canada in July, 2000.

Rebuilding

After a tornado strikes, many people have to start their lives all over again. Shops and factories can be completely destroyed, leaving people without jobs. Even the buildings left standing may collapse at any time. They are usually knocked down and cleared away with the rest of the mess the tornado has caused. Sometimes entire towns have to be rebuilt.

Disaster Detective

Can you think of anyone else who would be able to help after a tornado? How would they help? What sort of equipment might they bring with them?

Heavy machinery is needed to clean up the mess left by tornadoes.

Record-breaking tornadoes

The most tornadoes in one season

During the 1992 tornado season, 1,293 tornadoes touched down across the USA. In November of that same year, 94 tornadoes formed in 48 hours.

The longest tornado track

The longest tornado track recorded happened in the USA on May 26, 1917. It was 471 kilometers (292 miles) long.

The deadliest and fastest tornado

This was the tri-state tornado of 1925. It crossed three states of the USA and travelled 350 kilometers (220 miles) in three-and-a-half hours. It killed 689 people and injured 1,980.

The shortest, most damaging tornado

This tornado happened in Wisconsin, USA, in 1984. It killed nine people, injured 190 and flattened 100 homes in exactly one minute.

The highest number of tornadoes in one day

In the USA, Arkansas had 63 tornadoes in one day. This is three times the usual number of tornadoes they expect to happen in a year!

The biggest, most costly tornado

A series of tornadoes occurred in April, 1974 in the USA. It became known as the Super Outbreak, with 148 tornadoes in 11 states, killing 315 people, injuring more than 5,300 and causing US$600 million worth of damage. One of the tornadoes destroyed half a town, killing 34 people and causing property damages of more than US$100 million.

Glossary

anemometer	An instrument used to measure wind speed and direction.
atmosphere	A blanket of air surrounding the Earth.
clockwise	In the same direction as the hands on a clock.
cloud	A collection of water droplets and ice crystals in the atmosphere.
collide	To hit or crash into something.
condensation	When water changes from a gas to a liquid.
counterclockwise	In the opposite direction to the hands on a clock.
debris	Loose pieces of rock or other material that has been broken up.
dissipation	When the tornado has disappeared completely.
Doppler radar	Radar that finds the spinning air of a tornado inside a thundercloud.
dust devil	A spinning column of air that rises from a very hot surface such as asphalt. Also called a cockeye bob or willy-willy.
F Scale	The Fujita Pearson Tornado Intensity Scale. A scale used for measuring the severity of tornadoes.
fire devil	A spinning column of flames, ash and smoke created by the intense heat of a fire.
flash flood	A sudden rush of water during a thunderstorm.
funnel cloud	When the lower part of a thundercloud begins to swirl and drop down towards the ground.
gustnado	A small spinning tube of air at the front of a thunderstorm.
hailstones	Raindrops that are frozen inside the coldest part of a thundercloud before falling to the ground.
landspout	A spinning funnel of air and dust not attached to a thunderstorm.
meteorologist	A person who studies and forecasts the weather.
Northern Hemisphere	The northern half of the Earth, containing the North Pole.
radar	A signal that detects the distance, size and movement of objects.
radiosonde	A package of instruments attached to a weather balloon and used to measure weather conditions in the upper atmosphere.
satellite	A small spacecraft above the Earth that sends back information about the weather in different parts of the world.
Southern Hemisphere	The southern half of the Earth, containing the South Pole.
supercell	A long-lasting, powerful thunderstorm that can cause tornadoes.
TOTO	A weather station once used by meteorologists to study and measure tornadoes.
touchdown	When a funnel cloud touches the ground.
turtle	An instrument used to measure the wind speed of a tornado.
vortex	The spinning action of a tornado funnel.
waterspout	A spinning funnel of air over the sea.
wind shear	Winds blowing at different speeds and in opposite directions.

Index

In gratitude to the Fulbright Program,
whose generous support allowed me to conduct
the research for this book throughout Italy

To Suzanne Branciforte and Giulia Fera DiTommaso,
with heartfelt appreciation for their help
in translating the Piedmontese dialect

Thanks to David Gall, Deena Kaye, and especially
Heléne Alexopoulos of the New York City Ballet

All afternoon, the prince and princess talked. Then, when the sky had grown dark, she turned the pages of the book and changed the prince once more into a canary, which flew out of the window and slowly down through the treetops to the forest floor. She turned the pages back, and he became a man, who blew her a kiss before disappearing into the woods. The days that followed brought great happiness to the young man and woman, who, in time, declared their love for each other.

The queen, at her husband's insistence, came to see her stepdaughter a second time. Again she climbed the tower stairs and examined the room. She happened to glance out of the window just as the handsome young man came along the trail toward the castle. "Well, what have we here?" she thought. Moving closer for a better look, she saw an old vine growing on the outside wall, right up to the window ledge, which confirmed her suspicions. Overcome with wicked thoughts, she sent the girl to fetch her cloak. While the princess was gone, the queen snatched up the cushion on the windowsill and pushed several of her hairpins through it, so that the sharp points stood straight up. "There," she thought. "If he dares climb up here, he'll get a special welcome for his trouble." When the princess returned, the queen abruptly bid her farewell and departed.

The girl, impatient to be with the prince, who she knew would be outside, did not notice the hairpins in the cushion. She took up the book and anxiously turned the pages forward. The canary, as it had each day, flew to her sill. But this time, as the bird came to rest on the cushion, the pinpoints pierced its breast like spears. Blood began to stain its pale feathers, and yet the bird managed to rise feebly into the air and glide downward in slow swoops to the ground.

Terrified, the girl frantically turned the pages of the book, hoping the wounds would be gone when the canary changed back into a man. But it was not so. The prince lay on the ground, his garments soaked red, surrounded by his dogs, whose barking soon brought other hunters. The men picked up the prince and carried him off to his father's palace, more dead than alive.

The king could not cure his son, even with all the doctors and medicines his wealth could buy. The boy only grew worse each day. Word soon spread that the king would give anything to whoever could help his son, and though many tried, it seemed nothing would heal the prince's wounds.

By this time, the girl was desperate to know what had become of the young man. So, that night, she tried climbing down the vine outside her window, but it was too old and brittle. Instead, she tied her bed sheets together and slid to the ground. She ran and walked and ran again until she was so exhausted she had to rest. Leaning against a tree deep in the forest, she tried to sleep, but was too troubled with worries and fears.

At midnight she heard four loud whistles, one right after the other. From the darkness, four witches appeared, coming to this meeting place from the corners of the earth. The princess trembled and hid herself as best she could while the witches lit a fire. They warmed themselves a bit and then began to tell stories of what they had seen out in the world. Long into the night they talked, and the princess was nearly falling asleep when something she heard startled her. ". . .There's the son of the king from this land who lies dying because no one can cure him," said one of the crones with a laugh as she spat into the fire. "I alone know the secret to help him. For there, in his very room, under a tile in front of the fireplace, is a vial filled with an ointment that, if spread upon his wounds, would soon cure him."

The girl barely kept herself from crying out with joy. The witches finished telling their news with the dawn and took to the road once more. So, too, the maiden jumped up and set out for the town.

In the market, she traded her fine silk dress and velvet cloak for the tattered clothes of a poor shepherdess. Thus disguised, she went to the palace gate and begged the guards to let her try to help the prince. Seeing the girl in such shabby rags, they wanted to send her away, but the king overheard and said, "Many have attempted to help my son, and yet he suffers still. What harm can come from another try?"

Once in the room, the girl demanded she be left alone, and finally, her request was granted. Seeing her beloved so gravely ill brought tears to her eyes, but fighting them back, she remembered her task and searched the fireplace tiles for one that was loose. She found the vial and spread the ointment on all his wounds. As she touched each one, it was healed.

Filled with joy, she called the king, who marveled to see his son's wounds completely gone and color returned to his face. At once he offered the shepherd girl a fortune in gold, but she refused. She would accept only three things: the family coat of arms, a standard, and the bloodstained shirt the prince was wearing when he was hurt. Then she took her leave.

Soon the prince was once again out hunting. Passing the girl's window, he did not glance up once, for he was convinced it was she who had wounded him, and he no longer felt the same love for her. She was greatly saddened and let him pass; but when he next appeared on the trail, she could not bear his downturned head and at once seized the book and turned him into a canary, which had no choice but to fly up to her. Desperately she explained that the cause of his suffering was her stepmother's spiteful deed, and told him that she herself was the one who had cured him. But he did not believe her.

"It was a poor shepherd girl who saved my life," said the prince, "who took no gold for payment, but instead just three worthless things."

"Do you mean these?" She held up the crest, the flag, and the bloodstained shirt. Amazed, the prince fell to his knees, begging her forgiveness. She took his hands and declared her undying love. Then he asked her to be his bride.

That very day, he told his father of his decision to marry. The king, hearing that the bride was to be the young shepherdess, said, "Think well, my son, for you are expected to marry only the daughter of a king."

At which the boy insisted, "I will marry the one who won my heart."

The wedding day arrived, and all the kings and queens from near and far were invited. Among them was the princess's royal father, who knew nothing of his daughter's betrothal, for she had told no one. When the bride appeared, he cried out, "My daughter!" The princess embraced him and told him of all her misfortunes at the hands of his wretched wife, whom he immediately had seized and taken away to his dungeons.

The wedding proceeded with great joy and festivities, and
the happy young couple spent the rest of their lives together.